Bible Alphabets
ABC

Colourful Illustrations & Memory Verses

FOR

....

A is for
ADAM

The first man on earth

Genesis 1:26

Then God said, "Let us make human beings in our image, to be like us."

B is for
BIBLE
that tells the story of God

Psalm 119:105

"Your word is a lamp for my feet, a light on my path."

C is for
CANAAN

The Land of Milk and Honey

Deuteronomy 26:9

"And he brought us into this place and gave us this, a land flowing with milk and honey."

D is for

DANIEL

WHO WAS BRAVE IN THE LION'S DEN

Daniel 6:16-22

Daniel was brought and cast into the lions' den...but God sent his angels and shut the lions' mouths.

E is for
EARTH

The place where we live

Genesis 1:1

"In the beginning, God created the heavens and the earth."

F is for
FRIENDS

We are friends of God

John 15:14

Jesus said, "You are my friends if you obey me."

G is for
GOLIATH

WHO DAVID DEFEATED

1 Samuel 17:46

David said to Goliath, "This very day the lord will put you in my power and I will defeat you."

H is for
HEAVEN

A Happy Place Where God Lives

John 14:2-3

Jesus said, "In my father's house are many rooms...I'm going to prepare a place for you and I will come back and take you to be with me."

I is for
ISAAC

The Son of Abraham

Galatians 4:28

"Now you brothers and sisters, like Isaac, are children of Promise."

J is for JESUS

The saviour of the world

Matthew 1:21

"And she will give birth to a son, and you will name him Jesus, because he will save his people from their sins."

K is for

KIND

Doing nice things for others

Ephesians 4:32

"Be kind to one another, tenderhearted, forgiving one another, as God in Christ forgave you."

L is for

LOVE

The greatest gift of all

1 John 4:7

"Dear Friends, let us love one another, for love comes from God. Everyone who loves has been born of God and knows God."

M is for

MARY

The Mother of Jesus

Luke 1:30

And the angel said to her, "Do not be afraid, Mary, for you have found favour with God."

N is for
NOAH

WHO BUILT AN ARK FOR GOD

Genesis 8:19

And all of the large and small animals and birds came out of the boat, pair by pair.

O is for
OBEY

Doing the right things to please God

Ephesians 6:1

Children, obey your parents in the Lord: for this is right.

P is for
PRAY

How we talk to God

Philippians 4:6

"Don't worry about anything; instead, pray about everything. Tell God what you need and thank him for all he has done."

Q is for
QUEEN ESTHER

The queen that saved God's people

Esther 8:3

Then Esther spoke again to the king. She fell at his feet and wept and pleaded with him to avert the evil plan of Haman.

R is for

RIGHTEOUS

Becoming God's Child

Romans 10:10

"We believe with our hearts, and so we are made right with God. And we declare with our mouths that we believe, and so we are saved."

S is for
SHEEP

The flock that God leads

John 10:27

"My sheep listen to my voice; I know them, and they follow me."

T is for

TRUTH

What makes us free

John 8:32

"Then you will know the truth, and the truth will set you free."

U is for

UNICORN

Exalted Horn

Psalms 92:10

"But my horn shalt thou exalt like the horn of an unicorn: I shall be anointed with fresh oil."

V is for

VINE

Jesus is the vine, we are the branches

John 15:5

"I am the vine; you are the branches. If you remain in me and I in you, you will bear much fruit; apart from me you can do nothing."

W is for
WATER

Jesus is the Water of Life

John 7:38

"He who believes in Me, as the Scripture said, 'From his innermost being will flow rivers of living water."

X is for

XYLOPHONE

An instrument we use in praising God

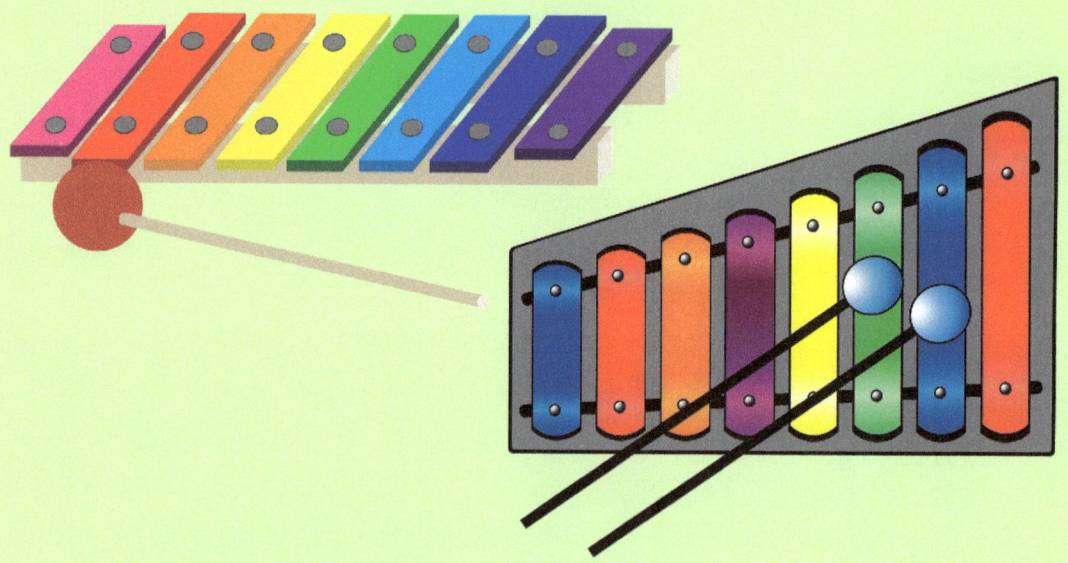

Psalms 150:4

Praise him with timbrel and dance: praise him with stringed instruments and the organ.

Y is for
yoke

WHAT KEEPS US TOGETHER WITH CHRIST

Matthew 11:29

"Take my yoke upon you and learn from me, for I am gentle and humble in heart, and you will find rest for your souls."

Z is for

ZION

The home of the blessed

Psalms 50:2

Out of Zion, the perfection of beauty, God has shone forth.

**WRITTEN BY:
ANTHONIA UDEMEH**

Copyright © 2021 by Anthonia Udemeh. All rights reserved.

www.ingramcontent.com/pod-product-compliance
Lightning Source LLC
Chambersburg PA
CBHW042256100526
44589CB00002B/41